BLASTOFF!

PLUTO

BLASTOFF!

PLUTO

by Rebecca Stefoff

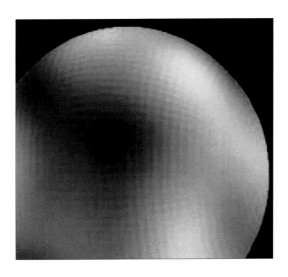

BENCHMARK BOOKS

MARSHALL CAVENDISH

NEW YORK

With special thanks to Professor Jerry LaSala, University of Maine,
for his careful review of the manuscript.

Benchmark Books
Marshall Cavendish
99 White Plains Road
Tarrytown, NY 10591-9001
www.marshallcavendish.com

Library of Congress Cataloging-in-Publication Data
Stefoff, Rebecca, 1951–
Pluto / Rebecca Stefoff.
p. cm. - (Blastoff!)
Includes bibliographical references and index.
Summary: Describes the history of Pluto, the ninth planet, and what has been learned about
it, and the current controversy over whether it is a planet at all.
ISBN 0-7614-1404-5
1. Pluto (Planet)-Juvenile literature. [1. Pluto (Planet)]. I. Title. II. Series.

QB701   .S83 2003   523.48'2-dc 21

2001006579

Printed in Italy
1 3 5 6 4 2

Photo Research by Anne Burns Images
Cover Photo: Space Telescope Science Institute/NASA/Science Photo Library

The photographs in this book are used by permission and through the courtesy of:
Bridgeman Art Library: British Library, 8; Kharbine-Tapabor Collection, Paris, 20; Prado,
Madrid, 29; Ludek Pesek/Science Photo Library, 34; Photo Researchers, Inc.: Sheila
Terry/Science Photo Library, 9, 11; Science Photo Library, 10, 13; Tony & Daphne
Hallas/Science Photo Library, 15; NASA, 35; Space Telescope Science Institute/NASA/Sci-
ence Photo Library, 26; David Ducros/Science Photo Library, 31; David Parker/Science Photo
Library, 32, 42–43; Jon Lomberg/Science Photo Library, 46; David A. Hardy/Science Photo
Library, 49; Victor Habbick Visions/Science Photo Library, 50; Lowell Observatory: 18; Julian
Baum: 7, 23, 25, 27, 39, 40, 45, 52, 55, 56, 57.

*Cover: The Hubble Space Telescope took this image of Pluto, which has been computer
processed to emphasize the contrast between bright and dark surface areas.*

CONTENTS

1
THE DISCOVERY OF PLUTO   6

2
PLUTO AND CHARON   22

3
AT THE EDGE OF THE SOLAR SYSTEM   38

4
PLUTONIAN PUZZLES   48

GLOSSARY   58

FIND OUT MORE   60

INDEX   63

1

THE DISCOVERY OF PLUTO

Billions of miles from Earth, on the far fringe of the Solar System, an icy globe about two-thirds the size of Earth's Moon slowly revolves around the Sun. This distant, little-known world is Pluto, the only planet to which Earth's scientists have not yet sent a space probe. Pluto was unknown to astronomers until 1930, and its discovery made headlines around the world. Alone of all the planets, Pluto was discovered in the daytime—and that is not the only odd fact about it.

SURPRISES IN THE OUTER SOLAR SYSTEM

Since ancient times, people around the world have watched the night sky and developed ideas about the Universe based on what they saw. They observed the rhythms of the Sun and Moon, which rise and set at different points on the horizon and different times of day throughout the year but repeat those cycles year after year. They observed the stars, which form patterns that move across the sky each night and change with the seasons, yet also repeat themselves yearly.

Ancient sky watchers saw five other bright objects in the sky. These points of light looked like stars but slowly shifted position

Artist Julian Baum's vision of Pluto with its moon, Charon, beyond it. The Sun appears as the brightest star in Pluto's sky.

against the starry background. They became known as planets, from Greek words meaning "wandering stars." Their names—Mercury, Venus, Mars, Jupiter, and Saturn—were those of gods and goddesses in Greek and Roman mythology.

For many centuries, Earth seemed to be the center of the whole Universe. In this geocentric, or Earth-centered, view of things, the Sun, Moon, planets, and stars revolved around the unmoving world

For centuries people believed that Earth lay at the center of the Universe. Early sky maps like this one, made by Andreas Cellarius around 1660, reflected this geocentric, or Earth-centered, view of the heavens.

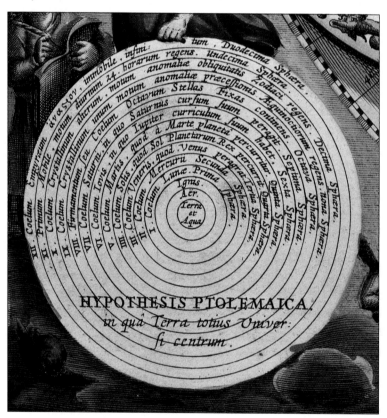

In 1781 William Herschel launched a new era in astronomy by finding Uranus. His discovery showed that the Solar System was both larger and more complex than anyone had imagined.

that is the home of humankind. Over time, however, astronomers found it harder and harder to match the observed motions of celestial bodies with the geocentric view. Eventually they put forth a new heliocentric, or Sun-centered, cosmology. In this view the Sun is at the center of a system of planets that revolve around it. Earth is one of the planets, and the Moon is its satellite. The stars are vastly farther away and do not belong to the Solar System at all.

By the eighteenth century the heliocentric view of the Solar System was known to be correct, and most educated people accepted it. They knew that Mercury is the closest planet to the Sun, followed by Venus, Earth, Mars, Jupiter, and Saturn. But in 1781 William Herschel, a musician and amateur astronomer in England, made a sensational discovery. Using a powerful telescope he had built, he spotted a seventh planet, a world more distant than Saturn. Christened Uranus after the ancestor of the Greek and Roman gods, Herschel's find was the first planet discovered since ancient times. It was proof

*After he became famous as the discoverer of Uranus, Herschel built this 40-foot
(12.2-m) -long telescope to pursue his real astronomical passion, the study of stars and galaxies.*

that the Solar System held surprises—and it soon led to still more
discoveries.

Soon after Herschel's discovery, scientists predicted the path of
Uranus's orbit around the Sun. They relied on Newtonian physics, a
system of scientific principles that English mathematician Isaac
Newton had outlined in the late seventeenth century. Newtonian

English mathematician Isaac Newton developed the theory of universal gravitation and the laws of motion that revealed the underlying order in the planets' movements—and led to the discovery of worlds beyond Uranus.

physics deals with the laws of motion, force, and gravity that govern all moving bodies, including planets and other celestial objects. To astronomers' surprise, Uranus's movement through the heavens differed somewhat from the path that Newtonian physics predicted for it. Scientists called this effect on Uranus's orbit perturbation, but they could not explain it. What could account for the fact that Uranus was not where it was supposed to be?

By the early nineteenth century some scientists had begun to think that Uranus's orbit was being perturbed by the gravitational pull of *another* unknown body in the Solar System, a planet even farther from the Sun. An English mathematician named John Couch Adams and a French mathematician named Urbain Jean Joseph Le Verrier tackled the problem. Basing their calculations on the difference between the predicted position of Uranus and its actual position, each claimed to have pinpointed the spot in the heavens where the unknown planet, too faint to be seen except through a telescope, could be found. In 1846 a German astronomer named Johann Galle sighted the new planet, right where both men had claimed it would be. After some squabbling about which nation deserved the glory of the discovery, the various people and countries involved agreed to share the credit. The eighth planet was named Neptune, after the Greek and Roman god of the sea, and scientists congratulated themselves on a job well done. At last they had solved the problem of Uranus's strange perturbations. Or had they?

THE SEARCH FOR PLANET X

In the year of Neptune's discovery, Le Verrier, one of the discoverers, suggested that still more planets remained to be found in the far reaches beyond Neptune. Le Verrier and others had discovered Neptune by studying the perturbations of Uranus's orbit, and he thought that a careful study of Neptune's orbit might reveal perturbations that would help pinpoint a new trans-Neptunian world. But Le Verrier added that such a study would require time, because Neptune creeps along very slowly in its orbit, taking almost 164 years to circle the Sun (nearly twice as long as Uranus). Le Verrier was right—after a half century of observation, scientists were not sure enough of Neptune's orbit to identify perturbations without doubt. However, there was another source of information: the old records of Uranian perturbations.

Scientists compared the expected course of Uranus with the planet's actual course, as recorded by various astronomers over many years, and then corrected the expected course by taking Neptune's gravitational pull into account. If the presence of Neptune had caused the perturbations of Uranus's orbit, the corrected course should have matched the actual course exactly. It did not. There remained a few tiny differences between the two—much smaller differences than

Bostonian Percival Lowell devoted his energy and much of his fortune to astronomy, although the scientific community ignored or rejected some of his favorite theories.

those that had led Adams and Le Verrier to Neptune. Astronomers began calling these leftover differences the "residual errors," or "residuals" for short.

Many experts believed that the residuals were simply the result of errors that many different observers had made while recording Uranus's position over the years. According to these astronomers and mathematicians, the residuals had no real meaning. A few investigators, though, saw the residuals as evidence that Neptune alone could not explain the motion of Uranus. Some of them began searching for a trans-Neptunian planet, trying to calculate its position by studying the Uranian residuals and also looking for signs of perturbation in the slowly growing body of information about Neptune's orbit. One of the most eager planet hunters was Percival Lowell.

Born in Boston in 1855 to a wealthy and prominent family, Lowell studied mathematics at Harvard University. After 6 years' work in his grandfather's businesses—enough to gain him a fortune—he devoted himself to travel, writing, and his scientific interests, chiefly astronomy. In 1894 Lowell built and equipped an observatory in the mountains near Flagstaff, Arizona, and hired a small scientific staff to carry out various telescopic surveys under his instructions. He spent most of his time in Boston and communicated with the astronomers by letter.

One of the astronomers' tasks was to look for a ninth planet beyond the orbit of Neptune. Lowell was determined to find this world, which he called Planet X because in mathematics "X" is often used to represent "the unknown." Every so often Lowell performed a new set of calculations, trying to identify the part of the sky in which Planet X could be found, and sent the results to Flagstaff with orders for the astronomers to search and photograph that region of the sky. In 1908 Lowell was disturbed to learn that astronomer William Pickering of Harvard, who had helped design the Lowell Observatory, was also using the residuals of Uranus to search for a ninth planet, although Pickering called the unknown world Planet O. (Pickering developed enormous interest in the idea of trans-Neptunian planets, predicting locations for some half a dozen of them, none of which has been found.) The competition spurred Lowell to expand his scientific staff and speed up his own search.

By 1914 Lowell believed he had correctly calculated Planet X's orbit and position. He was so confident that when he and his wife left Boston for a European tour he telegraphed the astronomers at his observatory, "Don't hesitate to startle me with a telegram— FOUND!" Alas, he received no such happy news. The following year Lowell presented his arguments in favor of Planet X to the American Academy of Arts and Sciences, but the members showed little enthusiasm, and so did the general public. Discouraged by Planet X's failure to appear, Lowell stopped speaking and writing

The Lowell Observatory near Flagstaff, Arizona. Percival Lowell founded the observatory in 1894. Today, much enlarged, it is a center of planetary studies.

about the trans-Neptunian world, although the search quietly continued in Flagstaff.

In late 1916 Lowell suffered a stroke and died while visiting the observatory. He left more than a million dollars in his will to the Lowell Observatory, enough to support its staff and its activities—including the ongoing quest for Planet X. Work was delayed for a

Lost in Translation

The Lowell Observatory's main task was studying Mars, which Percival Lowell believed was inhabited by a dying civilization. In 1877 Italian astronomer Giovanni Schiaparelli claimed to have seen narrow, straight lines on the surface of Mars. He called them *canali*, Italian for "channels." A channel can be a natural feature, but newspapers translated the word into English as "canals," which are artificial—signs not just of life but of intelligence. Fascinated by this notion, Lowell interpreted features on Mars as evidence of a planetwide civilization fighting an all-destroying drought. This romantic vision captured the attention of Edgar Rice Burroughs, creator of the fictional character Tarzan, who also wrote a series of novels about Martian cities, canals, and warriors, but it failed to impress the scientific community. Most astronomers correctly felt that Schiaparelli's *canali* were a blend of optical illusions and natural features, and they scorned Lowell's ideas about the Martian "civilization."

while, partly by World War I (1914–1918), but mostly by a long, drawn-out lawsuit in which Lowell's widow tried to challenge the will (she failed, but the effort cost the observatory fund large legal fees). Finally, in 1927, the astronomers in Flagstaff were ready to continue their work. They ordered a fine new photographic telescope, a gift from Lowell's brother, for the Planet X search, but the observatory's staff consisted of just three people—not enough to carry out all of its tasks. Director Vesto M. Slipher decided to hire an assistant to help with the quest for Planet X.

CLYDE TOMBAUGH SEARCHES THE SKIES

Director Slipher had a candidate in mind to fill the post of planet hunter at Lowell Observatory. He had received letters from Clyde W. Tombaugh, a young Kansas farmer, who had built several telescopes. The notes and sketches Tombaugh had made of his observations suggested that he was careful and thorough—two qualities needed for the Planet X search. Slipher wrote to Tombaugh and offered him a job.

Clyde Tombaugh had been born in Illinois in 1906. During his childhood he grew interested in astronomy because his uncle owned a small telescope and shared it with the boy. After the family moved to Kansas, Tombaugh remained spellbound by the heavens. As a young man he built several telescopes of his own, and by the age of twenty-two he was considering telescope-making as a career. Then he received a letter from Slipher offering him a job at The Lowell Observatory. With his father's advice ringing in his ears—"Clyde, make yourself useful"—Tombaugh set off by train to Flagstaff in January 1929.

Although Tombaugh had only a high-school education, he proved to be an excellent addition to the Lowell staff. At first he did all-purpose chores, such as shoveling snow and guiding tour groups. Then the new telescope arrived, and, after some coaching from

Clyde Tombaugh left a Kansas farm to join the search for Planet X at the Lowell Observatory in Boston. In 1930 he discovered Pluto—the announcement was made on the seventy-fifth anniversary of Percival Lowell's birth.

Slipher, Tombaugh took up the hunt for Planet X. His job was to photograph segments of the night sky through the telescope. Each piece of sky was photographed several times over the course of a week or so. Then the astronomers would compare the photographic prints to see whether one of the hundreds or thousands of tiny points of light had moved between the time the first and second prints were taken. A moving object could be a comet, an asteroid—or Planet X.

Tombaugh quickly proved that he was a skilled operator of the photographic telescope, and before long he was also entrusted with

How Pluto Got Its Name

After Clyde Tombaugh discovered the ninth planet, the Lowell Observatory received hundreds of suggested names for it. Constance Lowell, the widow of Percival Lowell, proposed calling it Zeus, after the leader of the ancient gods. Then she decided that such names were tired and old-fashioned and that Percival, or perhaps Lowell, would be a more suitable name for the new planet. Finally she came up with a suggestion she liked even better: Constance. None of her suggestions met with the approval of the Lowell staff, who had the right to name the planet.

One suggestion that the staff did like came from Venetia Burney, an eleven-year-old schoolgirl in Oxford, England. She felt that the planet should be named Pluto, after the Greek and Roman god of the underworld. According to Tombaugh, the Lowell staff was already considering that name when they received Burney's suggestion (and although no one remembered it at the time, a French astronomer had written in 1919 that if a ninth planet were ever found, Pluto would be a good name for it). In the end the Lowell Observatory astronomers named the ninth planet Pluto. Slipher said that its astronomical symbol would be the letters *PL*, Lowell's initials. However, William Pickering, the planet hunter who had been Lowell's rival years before, had the last word. When told of the new planet's symbol, he remarked, "That's a good name—Pickering-Lowell."

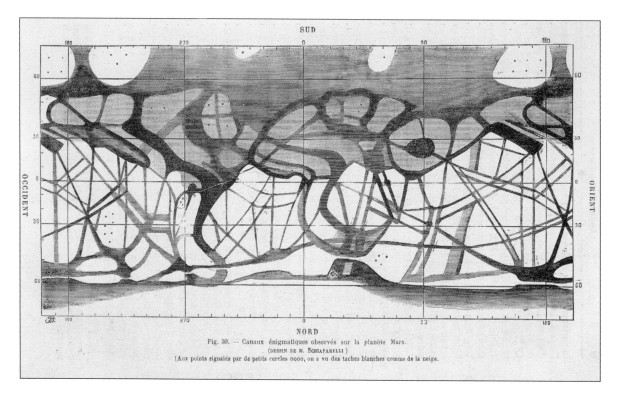

Italian astronomer Giovanni Schiaparelli thought he saw a network of channels on Mars. He drew maps such as this one, firing the imaginations of Lowell and others with visions of an advanced, canal-building Martian civilization.

the vitally important task of comparing the plates. He used an instrument called a blink microscope, or blink comparator, which holds two astronomical photographic plates. Looking through a special eyepiece, the operator views the two plates at the same time, and any difference between them appears to jump, or "blink."

Even with the blink comparator, the job was grim, as Tombaugh recalled more than 50 years later. On nights with clear skies and good visibility he spent hours photographing and rephotographing sections of the sky. By day he spent hours comparing plates, peering into the machine until his eyes swam and his mind grew so weary that he had to stop for fear of missing the telltale blink that would reveal Planet X. Tombaugh's search of the skies went on for months, during which he photographed and examined more than twenty-nine thousand galaxies and discovered two new comets. He did not give in to discouragement or despair, even when a visiting astronomer told him, "Young man, I am afraid you are wasting your time. If there were any more planets to be found, they would have been found long before this."

On February 18, 1930, Tombaugh was comparing images of the area around the star Delta Geminorum. He had taken two photographs on January 23 and 29. When he looked at them through the comparator, a faint star seemed to jump back and forth. "A terrific thrill came over me," Tombaugh later wrote. "Oh! I had better look at my watch and note the time. This would be a historic discovery." The time was four in the afternoon—the reason Tombaugh always said that he had discovered Planet X in the daytime.

For the blinking "star" proved to be neither a comet nor a flaw in the photographic plates. It was the long-sought ninth planet. But only on March 13, after the Lowell Observatory staff had made additional plates and examined them carefully to avoid any possibility of an embarrassing mistake, did Slipher announce the discovery to the world. The announcement was made on the 75th anniversary of Lowell's birth and the 149th anniversary of Herschel's discovery of Uranus.

2

PLUTO AND CHARON

The discovery of Pluto added a ninth planet to the Solar System and extended the Sun's family much farther into space. Yet even after Pluto was found, it remained mysterious. Ever since the Lowell Observatory published the big news about Pluto in 1930, gathering information about this faraway world has been a major challenge to planetary astronomers. Basic facts such as its size were extremely hard to obtain. Starting in the late 1970s, scientists used new and more powerful telescopes and other instruments to pry into the ninth planet's secrets, and in 1978 they made a huge step forward when they discovered Charon, Pluto's moon. Even before that time, however, investigators had patiently pieced together a few Plutonian facts.

FIRST PLUTO STUDIES

Once astronomers knew that Pluto existed and where to look for it, they combed the records of earlier observations to see whether someone had sighted it without realizing it was a planet. A number of such "prediscovery" sightings appeared in old observation notes and photographic plates. Ironically two photographs taken at the Lowell

One of the most exciting discoveries about Pluto was the finding of this large moon, Charon, orbiting the planet.

Observatory in March and April 1915, at the height of Percival Lowell's determined search for Planet X, had captured images of Pluto. They went unrecognized because they were much fainter than Lowell and others expected the ninth planet to be.

Prediscovery sightings of Pluto dated back to 1914. Together with the new observations made around the world after the planet's discovery was announced, these sightings let astronomers determine Pluto's orbit. Pluto revolves around the Sun once every 248 Earth years—which means that a year on Pluto lasts 248 times as long as one on Earth. Pluto orbits the Sun in what astronomers call 2:3 resonance with Neptune, which means that Pluto goes around twice in the time it takes Neptune to make three revolutions. This is another way of saying that Neptune's year is two-thirds as long as Pluto's.

Pluto's orbit has several unusual features. The orbits of most other planets are nearly (but not quite) circular. Pluto's orbit is an exaggerated ellipse, or oval. In fact, Pluto's orbit is so elliptical that for 20 years during every revolution it actually lies inside the orbit of Neptune. This occurred between 1979 and 1999, when Pluto was temporarily the eighth planet from the Sun, not the ninth. Pluto's closest approach to the Sun, which astronomers call its perihelion, came in 1989. Mercury is the only other planet to follow a highly elliptical path, and scientists do not yet know why the orbits of these two planets are so different from the others.

Because Pluto travels in such an elliptical path, its distance from the Sun changes dramatically over the course of a Plutonian year. At its farthest it is 4.62 billion miles (7.4 billion km) from the Sun, and its closest approach to the Sun is 2.77 billion miles (4.5 billion km). The planet's mean distance from the Sun—midway between its closest approach and its greatest distance—is 3.67 billion miles (5.9 billion km), nearly forty times farther from the Sun than Earth.

Another odd feature of Pluto's orbit is its tilt. The other planets move through space fairly close to what astronomers call the plane of

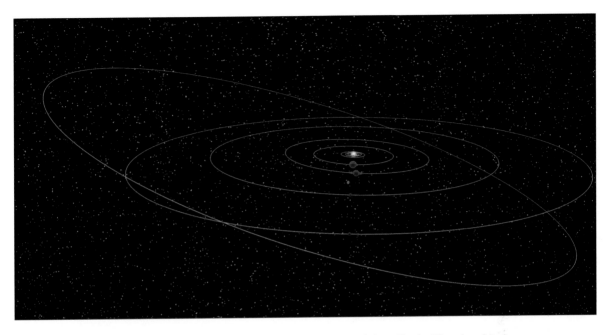

The planets orbit the Sun in a plane, or level array, called the ecliptic. Pluto's orbit, however, is tilted at a sharp angle to the ecliptic.

the ecliptic, an imaginary sheet stretching out flat in all directions from the Sun's equator. Pluto's orbit, however, is tilted more than 17 degrees away from the plane of the ecliptic. Instead of rolling around the Sun on the same general level as the other planets, Pluto is above the plane for part of each year and below it for the rest. The angle of Pluto's orbit, like the orbit's shape, is a scientific puzzle.

Compared with worlds such as Venus, Mars, and Jupiter, Pluto is dim as well as distant. At its brightest Pluto is visible only through telescopes, and it is about fourteen million times dimmer than Venus. In their book *Pluto and Charon*, astronomer Alan Stern and science writer Jacqueline Mitton explain that trying to study the planet's surface is like trying to examine a walnut that happens to be 30 miles (48.2 km) away.

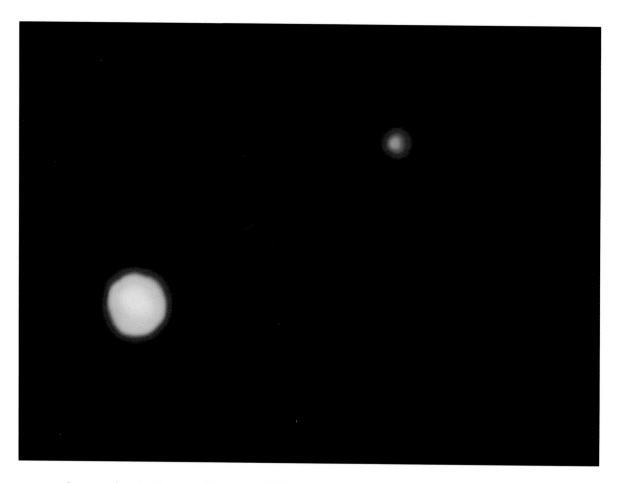

In 1994 the Hubble Space Telescope (HST) captured this image of Pluto and Charon—one of the best ever made of the ninth planet and its satellite. Pluto was 2.7 billion miles (4.3 billion km) from Earth at the time.

Pluto, astronomers decided, was too small and too dim to be a "gas giant"—a large planet with an extremely thick atmosphere, such as Jupiter, Saturn, Uranus, and Neptune, the other worlds of the outer Solar System. Pluto was more like the small, rocky inner planets: Mercury, Venus, Earth, and Mars. At first astronomers thought that

Pluto might be one-half or three-quarters the size of Earth. Then, in 1950 Gerard P. Kuiper, a leading expert on the Solar System, tried to measure Pluto with the new 200-inch (508-cm) Palomar telescope. He announced that the planet's diameter was no greater than 3,660 miles (5,890 km), less than half that of Earth. Since that time, astronomers have learned that Pluto is smaller than Kuiper thought—about one-sixth the size of Earth and two-thirds the size of Earth's Moon. Current measurements of Pluto's diameter range from 1,413 miles (2,273.9 km) to 1,485 miles (2,389.8 km).

Unlike the other planets, Pluto lies almost on its side as it revolves around the Sun. The broad red line indicates Pluto's equator, while the red arrow is the planet's axis, between its north and south poles.

Figuring out Pluto's period of rotation—the length of its day—was easier than measuring its size. In 1955 astronomers at the Lowell Observatory noticed that Pluto brightened and then dimmed in a cycle 6.4 Earth days long. The change occurred as the planet rotated, presenting brighter and then darker surfaces to Earth-based observers. This told astronomers that Pluto rotates, or spins completely around, once every 6.4 days.

DISCOVERING PLUTO'S MOON

In 1978 astronomer James Christy of the U.S. Naval Observatory was examining photographs of Pluto when he noticed something odd. In some photos Pluto seemed to bulge slightly, first on top and then on the bottom. Christy studied other, older photographs and saw that the bulge appeared on a regular schedule. He could think of only one explanation. A satellite must orbit Pluto. It was too close to the planet to be seen separately, but it was big enough to seem to stretch, or elongate the planet's disk. Pluto had a moon! Christy named it Charon.

Other astronomers soon verified Christy's discovery and added new information. Charon's orbit appeared vertical, rather than horizontal. Studies of Charon's orbit led astronomers to the insight that Pluto's equator is nearly vertical instead of horizontal. The planet's axis—the imaginary line running between its north and south poles—is tilted more than 90 degrees from its orbit. Instead of standing up and spinning like a top as it revolves around the Sun, Pluto lies on its side.

Charon revolves around Pluto in 6.4 Earth days and rotates on its own axis in the same period—which is also exactly the same as Pluto's period of rotation, a Plutonian day. Because gravity holds Pluto and Charon together in this pattern, which astronomers call synchrony, they always have the same faces turned toward each other as they move through space, the smaller whirling around the larger. Compare the Pluto-Charon relationship to the relationship between

The boatman Charon poles his craft across the River Styx, the entry to the underworld in Greek mythology.

Earth and its Moon. One side of the Moon always faces Earth, and the other side is never seen from Earth. Every part of Earth, however, faces the Moon at some point. There is nowhere on Earth where the Moon never appears. On Pluto, as on Earth, the satellite always shows the same face—but to only half of the planet. The other half of Pluto never sees the satellite at all.

One important result of the discovery of Charon was that, once astronomers knew the satellite's distance from Pluto and its period of rotation, they could use Newtonian physics to estimate the mass, or total amount of matter, of Charon and Pluto. They concluded that Pluto has about 1/450th of Earth's mass, while Charon is about one-fifteenth as massive as Pluto. Both worlds must be made of relatively light materials, without large amounts of heavy metals. Scientists now know that the Pluto-Charon mass is far too low to perturb the orbits of Uranus and Neptune. This confirms what many astronomers had long believed: Pluto was not the "Planet X" for which Lowell and others had searched.

Naming the New Satellite

Discoverer James Christy had the honor of naming Pluto's satellite. He wanted to name it Charon (pronounced Shar-on), a combination of the first syllable of Charlene, his wife's name, and the *-on* ending of scientific terms such as neutron. However, the International Astronomical Union, which oversees the naming of celestial objects, wanted the name to come from Greek or Roman mythology. Luckily Christy learned that Charon (pronounced Khar-on) is a character in ancient Greek myths—the boatman who rows the souls of the dead to the underworld. Charon was the perfect name for a satellite of Pluto, the god of the underworld, and it got Christy's wife's name onto the Solar System map, too.

An artist's portrayal of the Hubble Space Telescope against the Eagle Nebula, a distant cloud of gas and dust where stars are born. Earth's surface is reflected on the telescope, which has yielded the best images of Pluto.

TWO ICY WORLDS

New tools such as the Hubble Space Telescope, the Infrared Astronomical Satellite (IRAS), and supercomputers have made it easier for

The Infrared Astronomical Satellite, launched in 1983, was a valuable tool for astronomers. During its 10-month lifetime, the satellite surveyed 96 percent of the sky and discovered the existence of methane on Pluto.

today's planetary astronomers to study more distant objects than Herschel, or even Lowell, could have imagined. Although Pluto and Charon are still the least known of all planets and moons, some questions have been answered.

Scientists know, for example, that Pluto has an atmosphere. When the planet passes in front of a star, the star fades out of view and then back into view (if Pluto had no atmosphere, the star would disappear and reappear suddenly, not gradually). But Pluto's low mass means that it has low gravity. This in turn means that its atmosphere must be thin—the planet could not hold a thick atmosphere in place. Spectroscopes reveal nitrogen, methane, ethane, and carbon monoxide on Pluto. Experts think that these chemicals exist as ices on Pluto's surface. Small temperature changes as the planet rotates cause them to slowly vaporize into gases, creating a thin atmosphere that gradually bleeds off into space. Some suggest that the atmosphere exists only when Pluto's orbit approaches perihelion. When the planet moves away from the Sun, the atmosphere freezes back into surface ice.

Ice is a key feature of Pluto because the planet is a very cold place. Scientists do not yet know exactly what Pluto is made of or how it is structured, but they think it is about 70 percent rock and 30 percent water ice. Estimates of temperatures on its surface range from –378 to –396 degrees Fahrenheit (–228 to –238 °C). The coldest temperatures known on Earth are around –128 degrees Fahrenheit (–89 °C), recorded in Antarctica. On Pluto such temperatures would seem balmy!

Earth-based astronomers see Pluto as a spot of light, not a clear disk with visible features like the nearer and larger planets. Still, as early as the 1970s, a few astronomers tried to gain information about Pluto's appearance by studying its light curve, the regular variations in the sunlight reflected from its surface. Their work suggested that Pluto had a mottled surface, with a large light patch around its north pole and broad dark patches in the south. These findings were confirmed

Pluto as it might appear from the cracked and cratered surface of Charon.

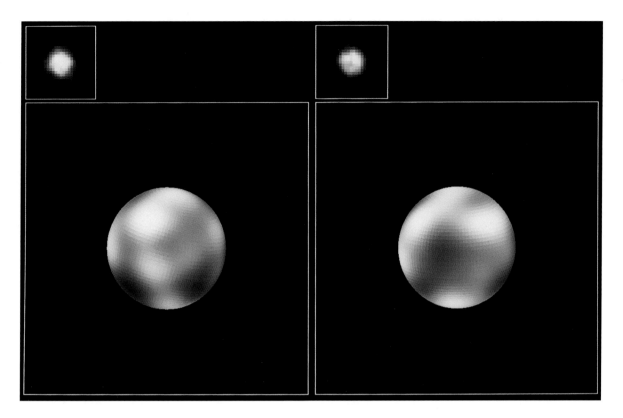

Pluto's surface shows considerable contrast between light and dark areas. The small upper pictures are actual images from the Hubble Space Telescope. The large pictures below are maps created through computer processing of the images.

and expanded upon in 1996, when astronomers saw the face of Pluto directly for the first time, through the Hubble Space Telescope. Images taken by the Hubble show that Pluto has more complex markings than any other planet except Earth and Mars—its surface is a patch-work of bright and dark blotches, some of them hundreds of miles or kilometers in diameter. No other planet shows greater contrast between bright and dark areas than Pluto. The bright patches are probably frost. The darker patches could be dust, carbon, or ice that

PLUTO AND CHARON FACT SHEET

	PLUTO	CHARON
Mean distance from Sun:	3.67 billion mi (5.9 billion km)	————
Mean distance from Pluto:	————-	12,400 mi (20,000 km)
Diameter:	Approx. 1,485 mi (2,389.8 km)	775 mi (1,247.2 km)
Period of revolution:	248 Earth years	6.4 Earth days
Period of rotation:	6.4 Earth days	6.4 Earth days
Mean surface temperature:	−378 to −396 degrees Fahrenheit (−228 to −238 °C)	unknown

has been darkened by chemical reactions with sunlight. The light and dark patches show clearly on maps made from the Hubble photographs by astronomers Alan Stern and Marc Buie.

Like Pluto, Charon is an icy world, although it does not appear to have an atmosphere. Astronomers believe that its surface is covered with water ice. One of Charon's most significant features is that of all the satellites in the Solar System, it is closest in size to its planet —about half the size of Pluto. (Earth's Moon, the second closest, is one-fourth the size of its planet.) Because Pluto and Charon are so much closer in size than any other planet-satellite pair, some astronomers think of them as a binary, or double, planet system rather than a planet and its moon.

3

AT THE EDGE OF
THE SOLAR SYSTEM

The discovery of Pluto drew attention to the trans-Neptunian zone, the part of the Solar System that lies on the far side of Neptune's orbit. Astronomers wondered how one small, rocky planet had come to be drifting alone beyond the realm of the gas giants. Then, in 1978 the discovery of Charon launched a new era of interest in the outer edge of the Solar System. Astronomers who took up the challenge of probing the trans-Neptunian zone learned that Pluto is not alone. The cold, dark outer Solar System is a surprisingly crowded place. Scientists now think that Pluto and other trans-Neptunian bodies may be survivors from the very earliest days of the Solar System, holding clues about how Earth and the other planets formed.

THE KUIPER BELT

Planetary astronomer Gerard Kuiper was one of the astronomers who focused on the trans-Neptunian zone after Pluto was discovered. In 1951 he suggested that space beyond Neptune might be filled with hundreds or even thousands of planetesimals, pieces of ice and rock left over from the planet-building stage of the Solar System billions of years ago. (Other planetesimals crashed into one another, gradually

Trans-Neptunia, the region beyond the orbit of Neptune, as envisioned by artist Julian Baum. Pluto is the largest known trans-Neptunian object.

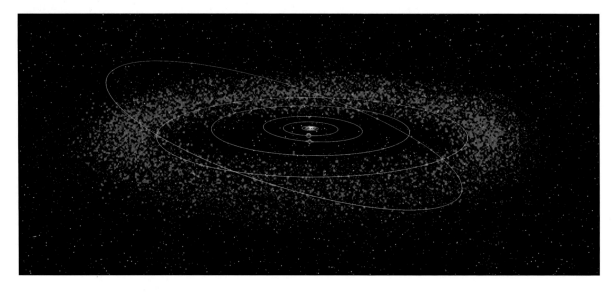

Astronomer Gerard Kuiper suggested in 1951 that a ring of rock and ice debris circles the Sun beyond Neptune's orbit. Later observations confirmed the existence of this ring, now called the Kuiper Belt.

building up larger bodies called protoplanets, or minor planets. Gravity then drew some of the minor planets together to form the planets.) Kuiper believed that a belt, or band, of planetesimals orbited the Sun beyond Neptune, but he could find no trace of it.

By the late 1980s new technology let scientists photograph the night skies with greater clarity. Several teams of astronomers began searching for the trans-Neptunian bodies Kuiper had predicted. In 1992 they found an object thousands of times fainter than Pluto orbiting the Sun beyond Neptune. Within a few years several hundred such bodies had been located. Known as Kuiper Belt Objects (KBOs), or Trans-Neptunian Objects (TNOs), they are among the most exciting recent discoveries in the Solar System. They are thought to be chunks of rock and ice, ranging in size from little more than dust particles to Pluto, the largest known TNO.

The TNOs that have been discovered may be just the first of many. Some astronomers think that the Kuiper Belt contains many thousands, perhaps millions, of objects. Billions of years ago, when the planets were taking shape, the TNOs could have merged to form a large world—but Neptune formed first. Neptune's strong gravitational pull drew many of the TNOs into its orbit, and Neptune swept them up and added them to its mass. Neptune could not capture all of the TNOs, however. Some were too distant or too small. Others, like Pluto, had orbits that never brought them within Neptune's gravitational range. Studying or visiting these surviving TNOs would be like traveling back in time more than 4.5 billion years, before the planets began to take shape in a slowly whirling cloud of gas, dust, and planetesimals. Planetary scientists could learn how various elements —including the carbon compounds that are the basis of life—were distributed in the raw material of the Solar System.

The Kuiper Belt is an enormous field of debris, or rubble, the unused building blocks of a planet that was never built. It is also a reservoir of comets, chunks of icy matter that follow highly elliptical orbits and display streaming "tails" of glowing gas when they are near the Sun. Astronomers think that many short-period comets, those that reappear every 200 years or less, come from the Kuiper Belt.

The Kuiper Belt is now thought to be not a narrow band but a broad, flattish disk that reaches outward from the orbit of Neptune, which is 30 astronomical units (AU) from the Sun. Some astronomers think that the outer edge of the Kuiper Belt is about 55 AU from the Sun, while others believe it could extend almost twice that far—although no TNOs have yet been spotted beyond 55 AU. With a mean distance from the Sun of 39.5 AU, Pluto's orbit lies well within the Kuiper Belt.

About a third of the known TNOs in the Kuiper Belt orbit the Sun in 2:3 resonance with Neptune, as Pluto does, circling the Sun twice for every three of Neptune's revolutions. Astronomers call these TNOs plutinos. The other TNOs orbit the Sun at varying rates, some

clustered in groups. The search for more TNOs continues, and it will undoubtedly bring surprises. In July 2001, astronomers working on a NASA survey of Kuiper Belt objects at the Cerro-Tololo Interamerican Observatory in Chile announced the discovery of a TNO about 4 billion miles (6.4 billion km) from the Sun. For now it only has a number— 2001KX76. Once its orbit is confirmed the International Astronomical Union will consider suggestions for a name. Thought to be between 600 and 785 miles (966 and 1,263 km) in diameter, 2001KX76 is about

The Cerro-Tololo Interamerican Observatory, high in the mountains of Chile in South America, is the site of a major survey of the Kuiper Belt that has already discovered a new object the size of Charon.

as large as Charon. It appears to be the largest object beyond the orbit of Neptune except for Pluto itself. The discovery led some scientists to speculate that the Kuiper Belt might hold more good-sized TNOs— perhaps even objects as large as, or larger than, Pluto.

THE FARTHEST FRINGE

After Pluto was discovered, its orbit was thought to mark the new outer edge of the Solar System—until scientists began finding other Trans-Neptunian Objects and uncovering the secrets of the Kuiper Belt. But does the Solar System have an outer boundary?

An invisible sphere or bubble called the heliosphere surrounds the Solar System. It is created by the solar wind, a stream of electrically charged particles steadily shed by the Sun. The heliosphere is the part of space influenced by the solar wind. Outside it is true interstellar space, which astronomers call the local interstellar medium (LISM). In this part of the galaxy the heliosphere consists mostly of widely spaced hydrogen atoms. The border between the heliosphere and the LISM, where the solar wind meets the flow of LISM particles, is called the heliopause. Scientists think that the heliopause is around 120 AU from the Sun, far beyond the planetary region and even the Kuiper Belt. The two *Voyager* probes, now heading toward interstellar space after surveying the outer planets in the 1980s, have picked up radio signals from the heliopause. They will probably reach it around 2010. If their communications equipment is still working, they may send back information about humankind's first step beyond the Solar System.

One part of the Solar System, however, lies far beyond the heliopause. Astronomers have never seen it or even detected it with their instruments, but they are fairly certain that it exists. It is called the Oort Cloud. Dutch astronomer Jan Oort noted in 1950 that many long-period comets, which take more than 200 years to make one circuit around the Sun, reach their aphelion, or farthest point from the Sun, at about 50,000 AU. He suggested that such comets come from a very distant collection of icy planetesimals. Scientists now believe that billions, perhaps trillions, of icy fragments surround the Solar System in a sphere or bubble outside the heliosphere. Called the Oort Cloud, this envelope of comets may stretch from 50,000 AU to as far away as 100,000 AU, halfway to the nearest stars.

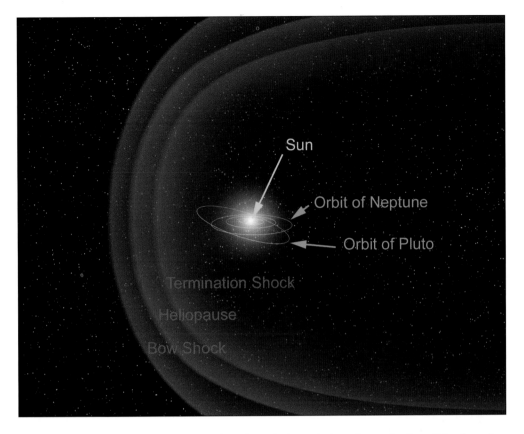

The heliosphere is a bubble created by the solar wind consisting of energized particles from the Sun. The heliopause separates it from interstellar space. Scientists call the point where the solar wind is believed to lose speed the termination shock. The bow shock is created by the pressure of the heliosphere as it moves through space, streaming away from the direction of the Sun's movement like water from the bow of a boat.

A few researchers have suggested that periodic tides or surges of energy in the galaxy affected the Oort Cloud in the past, shaking large numbers of comets into motion and sending them streaming through the Solar System. Perhaps the large bodies that struck Earth in the distant past, causing devastations such as the extinction of the dinosaurs,

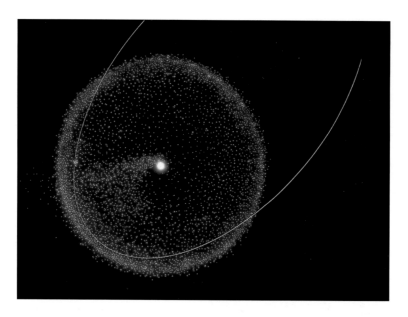

The Oort Cloud is thought to be a shell of icy fragments around the Solar System. A few scientists have suggested that the Sun has a companion star named Nemesis *(shown here in red). Periodically* Nemesis *might pass through the Oort Cloud, dislodging swarms of comets. No evidence, however, has been found to show that* Nemesis *exists.*

were comets jostled out of the Oort Cloud. For now, however, the Oort Cloud and its possible relation to the history of life on Earth remain mysteries.

IS THERE A PLANET X?

After Clyde Tombaugh found Pluto, he spent another dozen years planet hunting. As he admitted, he was "determined that if there were more planets to be found, they would be found at the Lowell Observatory." He found none and concluded that if more planets existed, they were small Plutolike worlds, very far from the Sun—a pretty good description of the recently discovered TNOs of the Kuiper Belt.

But what about Lowell's Planet X? Scientists know that Pluto cannot be Lowell's Planet X because the mass of Pluto and Charon together could not affect the orbits of Uranus and Neptune. The majority of experts today think that the residuals Lowell used in his quest for Planet X are simply mistakes and inconsistencies in the records of Uranus's position over the years. Uranus and Neptune are just where they should be. Luck and Clyde Tombaugh's hard work, not problems with other planets' paths, led to the discovery of Pluto.

A few astronomers, however, have disagreed with this view. Some believe that the residuals are accurate evidence of perturbations that must have been caused by an unknown planet. Others, noticing that some comets travel clumped together in clusters, have argued that the gravitational pull of a large unknown planet could have yanked them from the inner edge of the Oort Cloud into the Solar System and drawn them into groups. If such an unknown planet had an extremely elliptical orbit, it could now be far enough away from the other planets of the outer Solar System to be invisible, but during the eighteenth and nineteenth centuries it might have been close enough to perturb the orbits of the other planets. If so, its influence might not be felt again for a few hundred years.

Some of the astronomers who believe that a tenth planet exists have calculated positions where they believed it would be found, but all observations of those positions have come up blank. So have numerous searches of other photographic plates for a stray object that might be an unknown planet. Until Planet X is reliably observed and recorded, its existence will remain only a possibility. In the meantime, much remains to be learned about the known wonders of the outer Solar System: Pluto and its trans-Neptunian relatives.

PLUTONIAN PUZZLES

luto has always been wrapped in mystery. The years since its discovery have brought answers to some questions, but many new questions have arisen about Pluto. One debate that rages around Pluto is the question of whether it is even a planet at all.

IS PLUTO A PLANET?

Ever since 1930, diagrams of the Solar System have shown the Sun ringed by the orbits of nine planets. The orbit of the outermost planet didn't match the rest. It was oval in shape and cocked at an angle. But even if Pluto was a bit of a misfit among the planets, there was no doubt that it was a planet. Then, in the late 1990s, after the discovery of many Trans-Neptunian Objects circling the Sun in the Kuiper Belt, some astronomers rebelled against the decades-old classification of Pluto as a planet.

Scientists at the Smithsonian Astrophysical Observatory have questioned Pluto's status, as have others. The Astrophysical Observatory maintains records of bodies called minor planets. The minor planets include the asteroids, the Kuiper Belt or Trans-Neptunian

Asteroids, shown here in an artist's illustration, orbit the Sun like planets. The largest asteroids were once considered planets, and some astronomers now think that Pluto should be considered an asteroid or minor planet rather than a major planet.

An artist's portrayal of the Sun (background) and its family of planets, shown in their approximate sizes relative to one another. Tiny Pluto is at the upper right.

Objects discovered since the early 1990s, and a group of bodies astronomers have nicknamed "centaurs." The centaurs are asteroids or TNOs
whose highly elliptical orbits cross the orbits of the major planets.

Some minor-planet experts say that Pluto should be treated like the largest of the asteroids, which are bigger than some planetary moons. The first four of these big asteroids were discovered between 1801 and 1807. They were often called planets until the 1840s, when so many new asteroids were discovered that the Solar System was in danger of becoming ridiculously cluttered with scores of little "planets." At that time astronomers began calling them minor planets or asteroids, the names by which they are known today.

The minor-planet researchers argue that now that many Kuiper Belt Objects are known, Pluto should be recognized as one of them instead of being viewed as the ninth major planet. They point out that Pluto is very icy, like a KBO or a comet and unlike any other planet. Its orbit resembles that of a comet or a centaur. If Pluto were discovered today, they claim, both the International Astronomical Union and the worldwide scientific community would recognize it as a Trans-Neptunian Object and group it among the minor planets. Why, then, should we continue to call it "the ninth planet"? One astronomer was reminded of a story about Abraham Lincoln's riddle: "If you call a tail a leg, how many legs does a dog have?" Lincoln's listener answered, "Five?" To which Lincoln replied, "No, four—calling a tail a leg does not make it a leg!" Some would say that calling Pluto a major planet does not make it one.

On the other side of the argument are astronomers such as John Stansberry of the University of Arizona, who defines a planet as "any large, spherical, natural object which directly orbits a star, and does not generate heat by nuclear fusion." Stansberry's definition separates planets from comets and asteroids, which orbit the Sun but are not usually large enough to be pulled into round shapes by their own gravity. It also separates planets from stars, which produce heat of their own through nuclear fusion even when they orbit other stars. By Stansberry's standards, Pluto is definitely a planet. (However, this definition would also classify the asteroids Ceres, Vesta, and Pallas as planets, which most astronomers would be reluctant to do.)

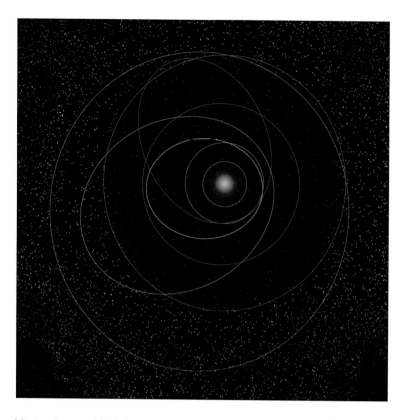

The trans-Neptunian world of the Kuiper Belt, seen from above in an artist's drawing, contains centaurs—minor planets whose oval-shaped orbits cross the orbits of major planets. Pluto's orbit is the outermost shown here. It crosses the orbit of Neptune twice.

Longtime Pluto researcher Marc Buie also considers Pluto a planet, not an asteroid or comet, because Pluto has an atmosphere and is round (most asteroids are lumpy and potato-shaped). Buie favors a three-part classification of the planets. Terrestrial or Earthlike planets would include Mercury, Venus, Earth, and Mars. Jovian or Jupiterlike planets would include Jupiter, Saturn, Uranus, and Neptune. The third category, perhaps called ice planets or Plutonian planets, would include Pluto and any other good-sized ice worlds in the outer Solar System.

The controversy over Pluto's status made headlines in 2000, when the Rose Center for Earth and Space opened at New York City's American Museum of Natural History. Astronomer Neil de Grasse Tyson, developer of exhibits for the center, included Pluto among the Kuiper Belt Objects instead of grouping it with the major planets. Some astronomers felt Tyson had gone too far in "demoting" Pluto. Others approved of his scheme, which organizes the bodies orbiting the Sun into five classes: terrestrial planets, the asteroid belt, the gas giant planets, the Kuiper Belt, and the Oort Cloud.

The debate over Pluto's planetary status has done some good by highlighting the complex nature of the Solar System and the recent exciting advances in planetary astronomy. However, the International Astronomical Union, which must approve the names and classifications

Plutomania

The Lowell Observatory announced the discovery of Pluto early in 1930. Later that year Walt Disney unveiled a new cartoon character, a floppy-eared dog who was the loyal companion of the popular Mickey Mouse character. Disney gave the dog a name guaranteed to get attention because it had been in the news a lot that year: Pluto. It seems that Disney either did not know or did not care that the mythological Pluto was the ruler of Hades, as the Greeks called Hell—perhaps a little sinister for Mickey's sidekick!

of all celestial objects, turned down a 1999 request from some astronomers to reclassify Pluto as a minor planet because so many other astronomers objected. Until the IAU changes its position, Pluto will officially remain what it has been since 1930: the ninth planet.

EXPLORING PLUTO

Many astronomers don't care whether Pluto is called a major planet, a minor planet, or something else entirely! They just want to learn more about this fascinating ice dwarf on the edge of the Solar System.

Researchers would like to know what the dark areas on Pluto's surface are made of. If, as some astronomers suspect, they consist of blackish carbon compounds, they might offer clues about how widely these compounds were spread in the raw material of the Solar System. That information might help scientists who are trying to figure out whether life is more likely to be rare or common.

Another question concerns the geology of both Pluto and Charon. Images available from Earth, or even from the Hubble Space Telescope, are not detailed enough to show mountains, valleys, and other surface features on Pluto and Charon—if such features exist. Scientists would like a much closer look at Pluto and its satellite. By studying surface features, they can see whether geological processes such as volcanic eruptions or earthquakes seem to have occurred on Pluto and Charon. This, in turn, would give clues to the internal structure of both bodies.

Astronomers would also like more information about Pluto so that they can compare it with Neptune's moon Triton, which is similar in size to Pluto and also contains a lot of ice. Because the two worlds are so much alike, scientists used to think that Pluto was also a satellite of Neptune at one time that somehow escaped the giant planet's gravitational field. Now, however, many think that Triton was originally a TNO in orbit around the Sun, like Pluto, until Neptune's gravity captured it.

Will planetary astronomers ever get that close a look at Pluto?

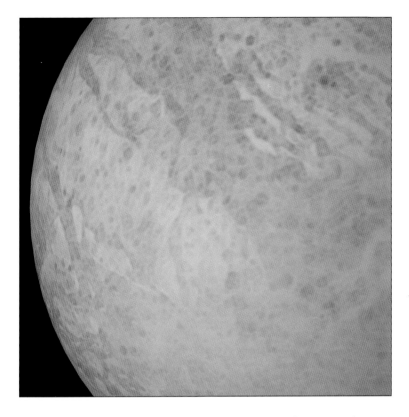

Pluto's mottled surface, visualized here by artist Julian Baum, fascinates planetary astronomers. Its dark patches could contain carbon, one of the building blocks of life.

Space probes have proved to be excellent tools for gathering information about distant worlds. Since the 1960s, such probes have approached or landed on planets, satellites, even asteroids and comets—but not Pluto, the farthest and hardest to reach of the known objects in the Solar System. During the 1990s, NASA began planning a Pluto mission. Teams of researchers designed a spacecraft called the *Pluto-Kuiper Express* to carry cameras, sensors, and communications equipment to the neighborhood of Pluto and Charon. In addition, the probe would be able to map and photograph part of the Kuiper Belt. If launched in

Pluto's interior is a complete mystery. Many experts think that the planet probably has a rocky core that may be surrounded by a layer of lighter rock or ice and a thin atmosphere.

2004, as originally planned, the probe would reach Pluto in 2012. However, by 2000 NASA had postponed the Pluto-Kuiper project because the agency's budget, granted by the U.S. Congress, did not contain enough money to pay for it.

A year later NASA began reconsidering a Pluto-Kuiper mission. NASA asked two teams of scientists and designers to come up with new, less expensive and more efficient proposals for a spacecraft to map Pluto and Charon, study Pluto's atmosphere, and carry out many other scientific tasks. Many astronomers, scientists, and supporters of planetary exploration have urged Congress to make money available for NASA to take the project to the design stage. They seemed to have won a victory in November 2001, when a congressional committee authorized $30 million for NASA in 2002 to design a 2006 mission to Pluto and the Kuiper Belt. Just a few weeks later, however, the administration of President George W. Bush announced that the mission would be canceled. Space scientists and supporters of

Does Pluto's surface resemble this vision of ice, rock, and a distant Sun? Only closer examination by a space probe can answer that question and many others about Pluto, Charon, and their trans-Neptunian neighbors.

exploration in the outer Solar System will try to win support for a later mission to Pluto, but scientists would like the spacecraft to reach Pluto before 2020. Pluto is now moving away from the Sun and Earth. Pluto is also getting colder, and at some point its atmosphere will freeze. The sooner the probe is launched, the shorter and cheaper the voyage will be, and the greater the chance of studying Pluto's atmosphere.

In 1991 the U.S. Postal Service issued 29-cent stamps featuring the planets, the Moon, and the spacecraft that had visited them. The stamp for Pluto showed a disk and the words "Not Yet Explored." Planetary astronomers and Pluto fans hope that those words won't be true for much longer.

GLOSSARY

asteroid   a small, rocky object that revolves around the Sun, mostly inside the orbit of Jupiter

astronomer   scientist who studies space and the objects in it

atmosphere   layer of gases surrounding a world; air

AU   astronomical unit, the distance from the Earth to the Sun (approximately 93 million miles or 150 million kilometers)

celestial   having to do with the sky, the heavens, or astronomy

cosmology   theory or image of how the Universe is structured

gravity   force that holds matter together and draws lighter objects toward heavier ones

interstellar   having to do with the distances between the stars

NASA   National Aeronautics and Space Administration, the U.S. space agency

orbit   regular path followed by an object as it revolves around another object

probe machine or tool sent to gather information and report it to the sender

satellite object that revolves in orbit around a planet; natural satellites are called moons

sensor instrument that can detect and record information, such as light waves, sounds, X rays, or gravitational and magnetic forces

Solar System all bodies that revolve around or are influenced by the Sun, including planets, moons, asteroids, and comets

spectroscope instrument that analyzes the light from an object to determine the chemical makeup of the object

telescope device that uses magnifying lenses, sometimes together with mirrors, to enlarge the image of something viewed through it

trans-Neptunian beyond the orbit of Neptune

FIND OUT MORE

BOOKS FOR YOUNG READERS

Brewer, Duncan. *The Outer Planets: Uranus, Neptune, Pluto.* Tarrytown, NY: Marshall Cavendish Corp., 1993.

Brimner, Larry D. *Pluto.* New York: Children's Press, 1999.

Daily, Robert. *Pluto.* New York: Franklin Watts, 1994.

Kerrod, Robin. *Uranus, Neptune, and Pluto.* Minneapolis, MN: Lerner Books, 2000.

Vogt, Gregory. *Pluto.* Brookfield, CT: Millbrook Press, 1994.

Wetterer, Margaret K. *Clyde Tombaugh and the Seach for Planet X.* Minneapolis, MN: Carolrhoda Books, 1996.

BIBLIOGRAPHY

Burgess, Eric. *Uranus and Neptune: The Distant Giants.* New York: Columbia University Press, 1988. This volume includes information about Pluto and summarizes the theory that the Solar System may include an unknown tenth planet.

Littmann, Mark. *Planets Beyond: Discovering the Outer Solar System.* New York: John Wiley & Sons, 1988. Revised and updated, 1990. This book deals with Uranus and the *Voyager 2* flyby of that planet, but also contains chapters on Pluto and the outer reaches of the Solar System.

Stern, Alan and Jacqueline Mitton. *Pluto and Charon: Ice Worlds on the Ragged Edge of the Solar System*. New York: John Wiley & Sons, 1998. A summary of recent discoveries and theories about Pluto and Charon, including a section on the development of a proposed Pluto probe.

WEBSITES

These Internet sites offer information about Pluto and pictures of the planet, as well as many links to other sites:

http://www.bbc.co.uk/science/space/solarsystem/index.shtml
Home page of the British Broadcasting Corporation's Solar System site, companion to a television series. One section of the site is devoted to Pluto.

http://www.seds.org/nineplanets/nineplanets/pluto.html
This Pluto site, maintained by the Lunar and Planetary Laboratory of the University of Arizona, is rich in facts, images, and links to related sites.

http://www.lowell.edu/users/buie/pluto/pluto.html
Marc W. Buie of the Lowell Observatory maintains this site, which is devoted to Pluto research.

ABOUT THE AUTHOR

Rebecca Stefoff, author of many books on scientific subjects for young readers, has been fascinated with space ever since she spent summer nights lying on her lawn in Indiana, gazing up at the Milky Way. Her first telescope was a gift from parents who encouraged her interest in other worlds and in this one. Today she lives in Portland, Oregon, close to the clear skies and superb stargazing of eastern Oregon's deserts.

INDEX

Page numbers for illustrations are in bold.

Adams, John Couch, 11, 13
American Academy of Arts and Sciences, 14
Ancients
    observations, 8
    and the planets, 8
aphelion, 44
asteroid, 18, 48, **49**, 50–52, 55
    asteroid belt, 53
astronomers, 6, 9, 11-14, 16-19, 21, 22, 24, 26–30, 33, 35, 37, 38, 40-42, 44, 47, 48, 50-51, 53–54, 56-57
astronomical units (AU), 41, 44
astronomy, 14, 17, 53

binary planet system, 37
blink microscope (blink comparator), 20–21
Buie, Marc, 37, 52
Burney, Venetia, 19
Burroughs, Edgar Rice, 16
Bush, George W., 56

centaurs, 50-51
Cerro-Tololo Interamerican Observatory, 42, **42–43**
Charon
    as binary planet system, 37
    discovery, 28
    exploring, 55–57
    geology, 54
    mass, 30, 47
    naming, 30
    surface, 37
    See also Pluto
Christy, Charlene, 30
Christy, James, 28, 30
comet, 18, 21, 41, 44–47, 51-52, 55

dinosaurs
    extinction of, 45–46

Eagle Nebula, **31**

Earth, 6, 8–9, 24, 26–27, 29-30, 33, 35, 38, 45–46, 52, 54, 57
    Moon, 6, 8-9, 27, 29, 37, 57

Flagstaff, Arizona, 14, 16–17

galaxies, 21
Galle, Johann, 12
gas giant, 26, 38, 53
gravity, 11, 28, 40, 51, 54

heliopause, 44
heliosphere, 44, **45**
Herschel, William, 9, **9**, 10, 21, 33
Hubble Space Telescope (HST), 31, **31**, 35, 55

Infrared Astronomical Satellite (IRAS), 31, **32**
International Astronomical Union, 30, 42, 51, 53-54

Jupiter, 8–9, 25–26, 52

Kuiper Belt Objects (KBOs), 40, 42, 51
    See also Trans-Neptunian Objects (TNOs)
Kuiper Belt, **40**, 41, 43–44, 46, 48, **52**, 53, 55–56
Kuiper, Gerard P., 27, 38, 40

Le Verrier, Urbain Jean Joseph, 11–13
local interstellar medium (LISM), 44
Lowell Observatory, 14, **15**, 16–17, 19, 21, 22–23, 28, 46, 53
Lowell, Constance, 19
Lowell, Percival, 13, **13**, 14, 16-17, 19, 21, 22, 30, 33, 47

Mars, 8-9, 16, 25-26, 35, 52
Mercury, 8–9, 24, 26, 52
Mitton, Jacqueline, 25

National Aeronautics and Space Administration (NASA), 42, 55–56
Nemesis, **46**
Neptune, 12–14, 24, 26, 30, 38, 40–41, 43, 47, 52, 54
    Triton (moon), 54
Newton, Isaac, 10, **11**

Newtonian physics, 10–11, 29
nuclear fusion, 51

Oort Cloud, 44–46, **46**, 47, 53
Oort, Jan, 44

Palomar telescope, 27
perturbation, 11–13, 47
Pickering, William, 14, 19
plane of the ecliptic, 24–25, **25**
Planet X, 14, 16-18, 21, 22, 30, 47
planetary region, 44
planetesimals, 38, 40–41, 44
planets, 8–9, 11, 24-25, 33, 38, 40-41, 46–47, 50,
    53, 55, 57
    defined, 51
    moons, 51
    names, 8-9, 12
    orbit shape, 24, 47
    order around the Sun, 9, 24
    three-part classification, 52
Pluto
    atmosphere, 33, 52, 56, 57
    axis, **27**, 28
    as binary planet system, 37
    Charon (moon), **7**, 22, **23**, **26**, 28–30, **34**,
        36–37, 38, 43, 47, 54-55, 57
    core, **56**
    discovery, 6, 21, 47
    distance from Sun, 24, 36, 41
    equator, **27**, 28
    exploring, 54–57
    geology, 54
    gravity, 33
    ice, 33
    mass, 30, 33, 47
    naming, 19, 53
    orbit, 24-25, 28, 44, 51
    perihelion, 24, 33
    period of revolution (year), 24, 36
    period of rotation (day), 28, 36
    planetary status debate, 48–54
    poles, **27**, 28, 33
    prediscovery sightings, 22, 24
    size, 26–27, 36
    spotting from Earth, 33
    surface appearance, 35, 37, 54, **55**
    surface temperature, 33, 36
    synchrony with Charon, 28
    viewed from space, **7**, **26**, **35**

visibility, 25–26
    See also Charon
Pluto and Charon, 25
Pluto-Kuiper Express, 55
protoplanets (minor planets), 40, 48, 51

residuals (residual errors), 13, 47
Rose Center for Earth and Space, 53

Saturn, 8-9, 26, 52
Schiaparelli, Giovanni, 16
seasons, 6
Slipher, Vesto M., 17–19, 21
Smithsonian Astrophysical Observatory, 48
Solar System, 6, 9v11, 22, 26–27, 30, 37, 38, 40–41,
    44–45, 47, 48, 51–55, 57
solar wind, 44
space probe, 6, 44, 55–57
    See also Voyager
spectroscopes, 33
Stansberry, John, 51
stars, 6, 8–9, 33, 44, 51
    Delta Geminorum, 21
Stern, Alan, 25, 37
Sun, 6, 7, 8–12, 22, 24–25, 28, 33, 40–42, 44, 46, 48,
    50, 51, 53–54, 57
supercomputers, 31
synchrony, 28

telescopes, 9, **10**, 12, 17–18, 22, 25
    See also Hubble Space Telescope; Palomar
    telescope
Tombaugh, Clyde W., 17-18, **18**, 19–21, 46–47
Trans-Neptunian Objects (TNOs), 40–44, 46–47,
    48, 50–51, 54
    plutinos, 41
    See also Kuiper Belt Objects (KBOs)
trans-Neptunian zone, 38, **39**, 40
2001KX76, 42
2:3 resonance, 24, 41
Tyson, Neil de Grasse, 53

U.S. Congress, 56
U.S. Naval Observatory, 28
U.S. Postal Service, 57
Universe, 6, 8
    geocentric view, 8, **8**, 9
    heliocentric view, 9
Uranus, 9–14, 21, 26, 30, 47, 52

Venus, 8–9, 25–26, 52
Voyager, 44
    See also space probe